Ethiopia
Grunsell, Angela

WORLDFOCUS

Ethiopia

ANGELA GRUNSELL

Contents

LINWOOD HIGH
LINWOOD

Introduction

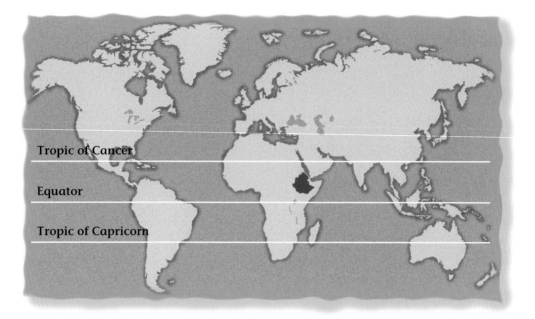

Tropic of Cancer

Equator

Tropic of Capricorn

What do you know about Ethiopia? You may have seen pictures on television of the terrible suffering of people during a **famine**, and this may be all you have ever heard about the country. What you may not know is that Ethiopia is one of the most beautiful countries in the world, with one of the oldest civilizations, and that you can buy trainers, pizzas and hamburgers in the capital city Addis Ababa.

△ **Where is Ethiopia?**

Contrasting lands and climates

Ethiopia is the most mountainous country on the continent of Africa. Almost three-quarters of the country is higher than Ben Nevis, the UK's highest mountain. In the central highlands mountains rise to over 4000 metres, split by countless deep gorges and valleys. Ethiopia has hugely contrasting climates. The Kolla are hot, tropical valleys. The Dega are cool, rainy highlands, where grain is grown and cattle graze.

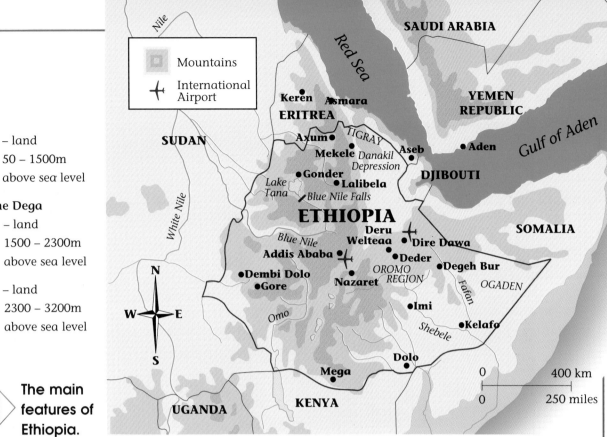

Kolla – land
50 – 1500m
above sea level

Woyne Dega
– land
1500 – 2300m
above sea level

Dega – land
2300 – 3200m
above sea level

▷ The main features of Ethiopia.

Map labels:

Nile, SAUDI ARABIA, Red Sea, Keren, Asmara, YEMEN REPUBLIC, ERITREA, Axum, TIGRAY, Aden, Gulf of Aden, SUDAN, Mekele, Danakil Depression, Aseb, Gonder, DJIBOUTI, Lake Tana, Lalibela, Blue Nile Falls, White Nile, ETHIOPIA, SOMALIA, Deru, Welteaa, Dire Dawa, Blue Nile, Addis Ababa, Deder, N, Dembi Dolo, OROMO REGION, Degeh Bur, OGADEN, Gore, Nazaret, Fafan, W E, Omo, Imi, Kelafo, Shebele, S, Dolo, Mega, KENYA, UGANDA

0 ———— 400 km
0 ———— 250 miles

▽ **Women working at the tree nursery in Deder, tending peach seedlings.**

The Woyne Dega, 'highlands of the vine' are high slopes where coffee is the main crop. Away from the mountains, the Ogaden in the southeast is a semi-desert plain: dry and bare. The low-lying Danakil Depression is one of the hottest, driest places in the world.

Plants and animals

In some parts of Ethiopia it rains four times the amount per year that it rains in the UK; in other parts it seldom rains at all. Rivers flow down in all directions from the beautiful crater lakes in the highlands into the valleys. The rivers are almost dry at some times of year and are torrents swollen by rain at others. In many places the rain is sudden and heavy, washing tonnes of topsoil a year off the land.

Ethiopia has a huge range of plants, birds and animals. Many are found nowhere else in the world. A wide variety of vegetables and fruit are grown. Although these are mainly food crops people grow for themselves, you may have seen Ethiopian beans or lentils as well as Ethiopian coffee in your local shops.

The people

A Christian Easter parade.

First human beings

Three million years ago the first humans probably lived in this part of Africa. Scientists have evidence for this from skeletons they have found in Ethiopia.

Early civilization

Ethiopia has been a crossroads of civilizations and peoples for thousands of years. The kingdom of Axum in the north was wealthy and advanced 2000 years ago when the Romans were ruling France and Britain. The people traded with Egypt and Asian countries. There were **Christians** in Axum more than fourteen centuries ago, long before there were Christians in northern Europe. Arab traders introduced the **Muslim** religion. Today about 40 per cent of people are Muslim and about 40 per cent are Christian.

Recent history

The steep mountains and valleys have had a big impact on Ethiopian history. Few outsiders have been able to conquer the highlands. The Italians invaded in 1895, but their army was defeated in Central Tigray and they kept land only in the north and along the coast.

The Ethiopian year is divided into thirteen months. This calendar is in Amharic and English.

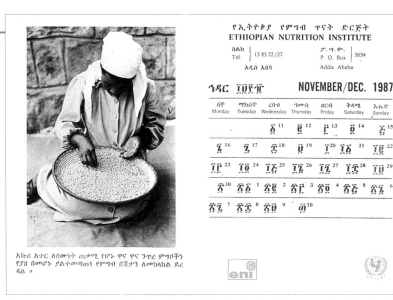

የኢትዮጵያ የምግብ ጥናት ድርጅት
ETHIOPIAN NUTRITION INSTITUTE
ስልክ
Tel. } 13 85 22/27
ፖ. ሣ. ቁ.
P. O. Box } 5654
አዲስ አበባ
Addis Ababa

ጎዳር ፲፱፻፹ NOVEMBER/DEC. 1987

ሰኞ Monday	ማክሰኞ Tuesday	ረቡዕ Wednesday	ሐሙስ Thursday	ዐርብ Friday	ቅዳሜ Saturday	እሑድ Sunday
·		፮ 11	፯ 12	፰ 13	፱ 14	፲ 15
፲፩ 16	፲፪ 17	፲፫ 18	፲፬ 19	፲፭ 20	፲፮ 21	፲፯ 22
፲፰ 23	፲፱ 24	፳ 25	፳፩ 26	፳፪ 27	፳፫ 28	፳፬ 29
፳፭ 30	፳፮ 1	፳፯ 2	፳፰ 3	፳፱ 4	፴ 5	፩ 6
፪ 7	፫ 8	፬ 9	፭ 10			

እኮሪ እተር ለስውነት ጠቃሚ የሆኑ ዋና ዋና ንጥረ ምግቦችን የያዘ በመሆኑ ያልተመጣጠነ የምግብ በሽታን ለመከላከል ይረዳል ።

eni

One of the 87 mosques in Harar, a very important centre for Muslims.

The highland and lowland communities developed separately. They have different dress, languages and foods. Although their population of 55 million is a bit smaller than the UK's, Ethiopians belong to almost 100 ethnic groups and speak more than 75 different languages. People have a strong sense of separate, local identity rather than seeing themselves as 'Ethiopians'.

The last 30 years in Ethiopia have seen almost constant political upset and civil war. Rebel groups in different regions have fought against central control. Emperor Haile Selassie, of Ethiopia, took control of Eritrea in 1952. This led to the formation of rebel groups who finally won Eritrea's independence back, in 1991. The Tigrayan and Oromo peoples also wanted independence and together became powerful enough to overthrow the unpopular socialist government in 1991. The transitional government, dominated by Tigrayans, has restored peace and promised more independence to eight new regions based on the country's main language groups.

Living in cities

In Ethiopia people live in cities and in the countryside. There are rich and poor people and people in between, but there is a bigger gap between the lives of the very rich and the very poor than in Europe. For example, a lawyer's daughter in the city of Addis Ababa might attend a private school, eat lunch in a restaurant and go shopping for pop-music cassettes with friends. Whereas a street boy, living with other children separated from their parents, might survive by selling matches to car drivers at traffic lights and persuading stall owners to give him left-over food.

Living in the countryside

Only one-tenth of Ethiopia's population live in the city or in towns, while in Britain three-quarters do. Nine out of ten people live in the countryside. Almost everyone farms the land. In the highlands and valleys families have small pieces of land on which they grow their own food. On the plains, **nomadic pastoralists** move around with their animals in search of pasture and water. They travel for most of their lives.

In the countryside you can clearly see how years of war and droughts in some places have ruined peoples lives. Ethiopia is a country recovering from difficult times. Life is hard for most farming families. Producing enough food in a year just for themselves is a worry. Few people have piped water and more than half live over six miles from the nearest health centre.

Crowds and traffic in downtown Addis Ababa.

 There's a wide choice of shoes on sale in town markets.

Grazing cattle in the highlands.

In the past, under Haile Selassie, poorer people got the worst pieces of ground to farm, while landowners made money out of the best land. When the rains failed in 1973, drought brought **famine** to the poor and over 200,000 people died. The **Derg** government **nationalized** land and at first people were happy about this. But, after the 1983 famine, the government forced thousands of people to move to new areas where they might be able to grow enough food to live on. The government hoped to reduce the burden on over-farmed areas. New villages were built and people had to live alongside strangers. The government put up taxes and made everyone work for the community for free on one day a week. Now the new government wants to give people more control over their lives. Many people are returning to their old areas. New laws give them the right to use this land and pass it on to their children.

Agriculture

Subsistence farming

Most of the crops in Ethiopia are food crops grown by people for themselves. This is called subsistence farming. People grow different foods according to the weather and customs where they live. In the low, hot lands – the Kolla – people grow **sorghum** (which takes about eight months to ripen). Farmers in the cool, high mountains – the Dega – grow wheat and barley. On the middle slopes, **teff** is grown, Ethiopia's most popular grain for making **injera**, a dark, soft, spongy bread. On the semi-desert plains there is not enough rain to grow crops at all so people there keep flocks of sheep and goats. They buy the grain they need to make bread with money from selling their animals.

▽ Oxen pulling a plough to break up the soil.

This boy, aged seven, takes cows to graze on the hillside all day.

Everyone in the family helps with farming work as soon as they are old enough to do a bit of weeding or to feed the chickens. From the age of about eight, boys go out into the hills for the day in small groups, with all the sheep or cattle of a village. Girls help with the harvest.

People need money to pay for clothes, medicines and school books. Children sometimes walk many miles to the weekly market in the nearest town to sell a chicken, some vegetables or spices or to buy things like soap, matches and candles for the family.

Cash crops

But some crops are grown for **export** to other countries. Coffee, grown all over the highlands, is the main **cash crop**. It needs good light soil and plenty of water. Coffee got its name from the Kaffa region of Ethiopia where it has been grown and drunk for thousands of years. The price of coffee is fixed by the international market, so how much money farmers get for their coffee depends on how much coffee is being grown and drunk worldwide.

A Jinka coffee grower with freshly picked coffee beans.

Another cash crop is chat, a leaf which people chew. It is a mild stimulant, used rather like alcohol in the West. There is great demand for chat in Somalia and in the **Muslim** countries across the Red Sea. Hides and skins from the **pastoralists'** flocks on the plains are also exported to other countries.

9

Industry

Mineral resources

Ethiopia has natural mineral resources such as iron, zinc, copper and gold. Large-scale mining of gold has begun. If the government is successful in attracting foreign businesses to invest in Ethiopia there will be good prospects for exporting other minerals too. These **primary industries** could employ people who have come to the towns and cities looking for work.

▷ Axum's tallest carved pillar is 23 metres high. It has 'windows' and 'doors' on ten 'floors'.

Consumer goods

Most manufacturing industry is on quite a small scale, but there are large factories and workshops in Addis Ababa, Dire Dawa and Nazaret. These make consumer goods for people in Ethiopia to buy: things like matches, cigarettes and beer. Fruit is canned, and sells to richer people. Cotton grown in the country is made into clothes. Some international companies, like Pepsi Cola, have **franchized** factories.

▽ Pepsi Cola factory in Addis Ababa.

Transport

It is not surprising that a country where travel by land is so difficult has one of the most successful airlines in Africa. A big network of internal flights can cover distances in two hours that take days by bus and weeks on foot. *Ethiopian Airlines* also runs flights to many other countries, especially in Africa.

In every town, expert motor mechanics in small workshops repair trucks and cars worn out by the rough mountain roads and long distances. Medlin Gerziger, a 23-year-old woman mechanic says: '*I can fix any vehicle, whether it's a Fiat, a Toyota or a Mercedes truck.*'

Tourism

Ethiopia's tourist industry is starting again. People can visit ancient monuments like the carved stone pillars at Axum and the medieval churches at Lalibela and Gonder. The Blue Nile falls and Lake Tana are famous beauty spots. Sidamo on the borders of Kenya could be developed as a safari region. There have been high-rise luxury hotels belonging to international chains in Addis Ababa for decades. A thriving tourist industry gives people jobs, but it does not bring a great deal of money into a country, because many of the supplies used are **imported**.

Challenges

Producing enough food to feed everyone

For centuries, Ethiopians have farmed their land and fed themselves. They have managed in a difficult climate where rains are unpredictable and there have been droughts every few years. Now, with a more open government and a return to peace, the fields are full of people ploughing and planting without fear of attack, in some areas for the first time in years.

Houses are being built in every town and village. Refugees are coming back from Sudan and Somalia and soldiers are returning to their homes.

Ethiopians grow enough food to meet about 85 per cent of the country's food needs. The rest comes from **food aid** from other countries and **imported** food. The challenge is to reach a point where there is enough food produced to feed everyone.

◁ Thousands of soldiers are returning home. This man is earning a living keeping bees and selling honey.

△ Cutting five-year-old eucalyptus saplings at a new tree plantation.

Replanting the forests

The country and its farmers face another big challenge: damage to the environment through loss of trees and topsoil. Until the Second World War almost half of Ethiopia was covered with forest. Now, 50 years later, only 2 or 3 per cent remains. This is because trees are used for firewood, for cooking and heating, and in some areas have been cleared to make way for the crops needed to feed a larger population.

Where animals have eaten the grass and many trees have been cut down, there are no roots to hold the soil together. The soil can be blown away by the wind or washed away when the rains come. Now people are having to plant and care for new trees as part of farming. Umar, from the Eastern Highlands explains, *'We have brought the land back to life by planting trees. Trees help keep soil wet so that more food can be grown. Trees can be harvested like a crop.'* Jundi Ame from Oromo sees tree planting as a long term way of improving things, *'I'm planting trees so that when my children grow up they'll be able to build their own houses and have fuel.'*

A farming community

Deru Welteaa: the place

Deru Welteaa Peasants Association is in the Oromo Region. It is in an area of green hills and valleys between the hot lowlands and the cooler highlands. It is east of Addis Ababa and about 200 km south of Dire Dawa, Ethiopia's second largest city.

Most people living in Deru Welteaa will never have visited these places. The place that really matters to them is the market town of Deder, only 2 km away. That's where the school, the doctor's clinic and the hospital are. It takes about half an hour to walk there and most people have to walk. There is no all-weather road for vehicles – the road is dusty when it's dry and muddy when it rains. But you would always meet people you know along the way. It's safe for adults and children as young as seven to go backwards and forwards without worrying about being mugged or knocked down. But a better road is something everyone wants.

▷ The community of Deru Welteaa.

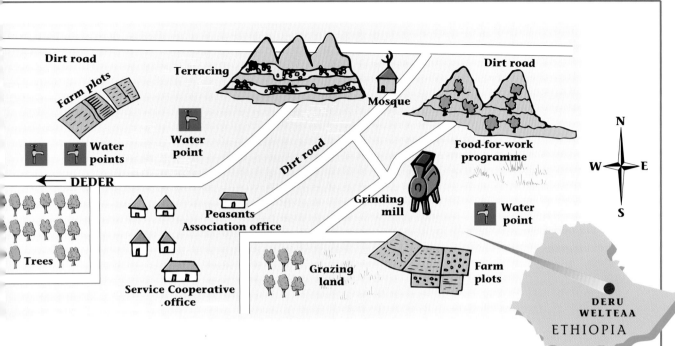

Dirt road

Terracing

Farm plots

Mosque

Dirt road

Water points

Water point

Food-for-work programme

Dirt road

← DEDER

Grinding mill

Water point

Trees

Peasants Association office

Service Cooperative office

Grazing land

Farm plots

N
W E
S

DERU WELTEAA
ETHIOPIA

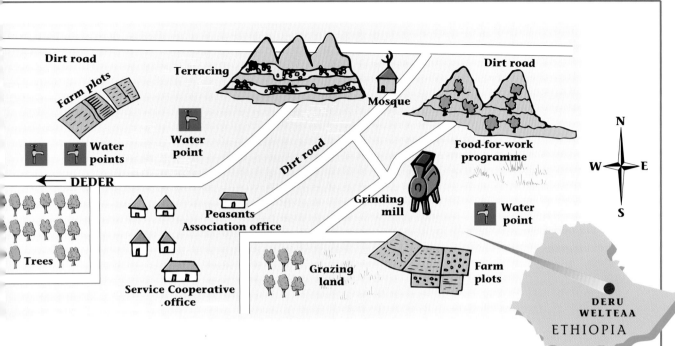
△ A shop in Deder town, where people can buy batteries or Pepsi Cola.

◁ Farms are scattered among the fields and slopes.

Deru Welteaa: the people

Fifty families live in Deru Welteaa. The previous government built the houses to encourage people to live closer together instead of on separate farms. Some families still live in small farms scattered around the valley. There is a Peasants Association office, which also acts as a post office, and a mill which makes flour out of local corn. There is also a **Service Cooperative** shop set up by the government which sells basic food supplies, kerosene for cooking stoves, clothes, pens and paper. The shop also sells farm tools at a cheap price. There are now three improved water points, places to collect clean water, in Deru Welteaa. These have made a big difference to the lives of women and children whose job it is to collect it. Now they do not have far to walk if they live in the village.

As well as growing vegetables and grain on their own plots of land, people work together on 'Food for Work' activities supported by Oxfam. Oxfam provides a fixed quantity of food per day for an agreed amount of work done to help everyone in the neighbourhood. People work on set projects for two to three months a year, in the winter time after harvest. One project is to dig terraces into the hillsides so that precious rain does not wash away topsoil, but sinks into the ground helping the vegetables and **sorghum** there to grow.

Village life

Religion

Most people in Deru Welteaa are **Muslims**. There is a small mosque near the grinding mill in Deru Welteaa with an Islamic crescent on the roof. Most of the men go to pray there on Fridays.

Weather and pests

The weather in this region is mostly hot and dry. Between July and September is the main wet season, when dusty paths and hillsides turn into fast-flowing streams and mud overnight. Just as suddenly, the hillsides turn green and flowers bloom. Rains come again in March or April, but when or how much there will be no-one knows. If the rains are late or too short to soak the ground, crops do not grow well. Pests are also a problem. If locusts attack the green shoots of the growing **sorghum** crop in June, July and August there won't be enough of a harvest to keep families going until the next year.

▽ Building a check dam, to prevent storm rains washing away precious top soil.

△ Four-year-old boy helping his parents with weeding.

▷ Mohamed Nour loading tree seedlings at Ganda Dagre tree nursery onto his donkey. He will plant them near to the village.

Homes and housework

Most families live in **tukuls**. These are small round houses made from eucalyptus wood frames. A central pole holds up the thatched roof and the walls are made of a mud and straw plaster called chika. The houses in the village around the office and shop are square with roofs made of corrugated iron sheeting and walls made of chika. Men, women and children each have some special jobs and share others. Everyone plays a part in looking after the family crops and animals. Women and children collect the firewood and water needed for the cooking.

School

△ Children in a Primary school in Dimeka, southern Ethiopia.

Getting to school

Over half the children aged between seven and eleven in Deru Welteaa go to the primary school in Deder. They have five hours of school just like children in the UK, but it is all in the morning. The children walk to school, starting at 7 a.m. to be there for 7.30 a.m. If they are only at the top of the last hill when they hear the teacher's whistle for line-up, everyone stampedes the last stretch to make it in time. When it's wet, they carry their shoes so as not to get them muddy and put them on just outside school.

What do they learn?

At school the children learn three languages. How many children do you know who can speak three languages? Their most important language is Oromifaa, which is the language of their people, the Oromo. They speak it at home. The second is Amharic, which is spoken by all the different ethnic groups in Ethiopia and is the language of signs and textbooks. Their third language is English. They learn the history and geography of their country. They are also taught science, maths and health education. There is a secondary school in Deder but not many children continue with formal education after primary school.

The Qu'ran school

Some children, mostly boys but some girls, attend **Qu'ran** school at the mosque instead of going to primary school in Deder. Here they learn about the **Muslim** religion, Arabic writing, what to wear and how to behave as a Muslim.

Who doesn't go to school?

Many children don't go to school. Education for them is learning to do what the grown-ups have to do, and finding people who can teach them the things they need to know, when they have got the time. Many families don't have the spare cash to buy pencils, exercise books and the kinds of clothes children have to wear at school. Other families need everyone to help around the house and with farming. Girls often have to look after younger brothers and sisters at home.

Parents want schooling for their children, but (as in the UK) they worry about the future, *'There is more and more unemployment, especially in the towns, but also in the countryside. Young people have nothing to do after all the effort they have made to get an education. It's a case of education for what?'*

▽ **These children in Lalibela are just a few of the 75 per cent of children who don't have the chance to go to school.**

Spare time

Children in the countryside around Deder have to work hard, but when they have time to play they have lots of space and freedom. They usually have plenty of company too, whether they are going to town, minding younger brothers and sisters or herding animals.

Expeditions, like going for water or gathering wood, usually involve a group of children together, so there is joking and play along the way. Children spend most of their time outdoors and they make up the kinds of games that children play everywhere: mothers-and-fathers, chase games and jumping games. Boys play football on the slopes with small cloth balls when the sheep are getting on with grazing. Girls play clapping games and sing lots of songs, the way children do in European playgrounds.

▷ Meftuha Mohamed collecting water.

Women

No one has much spare time – especially women, with all the extra work on top of farming they have to do to prepare the family's meals. This means they not only collect wood and water, but also grind grain into flour they may need, and milk the cow – all before they start cooking. But like the children, the women often go about their work together. Sometimes in the hottest part of the day, the early afternoon, the women in neighbouring houses get together for an hour or so to drink coffee and talk in the cool of the house. Some bring baskets they are making or clothes to mend while the coffee is prepared.

△ Young children in a school playground, in Hamar, southern Ethiopia.

Men

Men, especially younger men without land to farm, have more spare time. There is a shortage of land to farm which can be divided between the younger men in Deru Welteaa. Some of them can only get work in the Food for Work projects and can't find regular work at other times. They get together in the village in the afternoons and evenings, and sit talking and chewing Chat.

City entertainments

In Addis Ababa and Dire Dawa, for those who have the money, there are restaurants and cinemas. Children of wealthy families can go to private sports clubs after school where they can play tennis or swim in the pool. There is television to watch in the evenings.

A day with Ayoob and Fa'te

Ayoob and Fa'te are not real children. They have been made up to give an idea of what life is like for the children of Deru Welteaa. Ayoob and Fa'te sleep on a mattress of hay on the floor of their family **tukul** with their family. They sleep on one side of the room and the animals sleep on the other. The first sounds they hear in the morning are the cocks crowing in the village at dawn. It is November and the morning air is cool and fresh, but the sun will be hot and fierce by midday.

Breakfast

Fa'te helps her mother get the fire going for breakfast. They clear and tidy the mattresses to sit on. Breakfast is a mixture made from last night's meal. It is **injera**, made from **sorghum** mixed with a little **teff**, chopped and quickly cooked in a light sauce thickened with a little sweet potato. Everyone drinks hodja, made by boiling coffee leaves with a few coffee beans and salt in water, with milk added afterwards. Before going to school Ayoob takes the family cow, ox and goats outside the tukul.

△ This family, Safia, Ahmed and their son, live near Deder. Ahmed works as a tree guard.

On the way home from school, with their friends, the children stop off to get a drink of water from a pond not far from the road. They often play for a while before going to their separate homes.

Once home Ayoob cuts a piece of sugar cane to suck from the family field. It is sweet and delicious. The family don't have a meal at lunchtime, but the children and their mother drink more hodja. Their father makes hodja out in the fields where he is weeding. Ayoob takes the animals to graze up the hill. Other boys have been there since morning. Fa'te helps her mother to fetch the water and collect more kindling wood. They usually go with her cousins and their mother.

△ Planting a seedling from the tree nursery.

The end of the day

At dusk the family get together to eat the evening meal of injera with boiled cabbage and sweet potato. Sometimes they have porridge made from maize flour, which is thick and tasty. The family only eat meat at special times, like the Islamic holiday Eid after Ramadan. Most villages do not have electricity so the family gather round the light from the fire to talk about the day. Many families listen to the Oromo hour on the radio in the evenings. Everyone goes to bed at much the same time, around 8 p.m., because they will all be up early tomorrow, woken by the cocks crowing at dawn.

Travelling to Deder

Improving the roads

The road from Deru Welteaa to Deder is being improved by young men working on the Food for Work project. Rocks are used to give the road better drainage in wet weather. At present it is impossible for pick-up trucks to get through when it rains. Supplies of soap and salt run out at the shop, because they cannot be transported, although some are brought in on donkeys. If someone has an accident they have to be carried to Deder for the half-hour journey on a stretcher by neighbours. If a small child is sick and needs to be taken to the clinic, their mother has to carry them all the way.

△ Setting out for Deder market in new clothes bought for the Islamic hoilday, Eid.

◁ The road to Deder.

Market day

Once a week, women and some of the children from Deru Welteaa go to the weekly market in Deder. They take eggs, butter, vegetables and baskets they have made to sell. Not every family has a donkey, but if anyone has a donkey she will let other women use it too. On the return journey they bring as much salt, coffee and matches, sugar and kerosene as they can carry between them. Sometimes everything they have taken gets sold, but not always.

Although a vehicle is a rare sight on the roads from Deru Welteaa, there are plenty of taxis, mini buses and trucks on the streets of Deder. They provide transport between Deder and the town of Kobo on the main road to Addis Ababa and Dire Dawa.

▽ Asheref Hassan has carried her sick child all the way to Deder.

Travelling in Ethiopia

The easiest way to cover Ethiopia's ground is by air, but that is much too expensive for most people.

△ A small plane for internal flights does not need a long runway.

Railways

There is a railway from Djibouti Port, on the Red Sea coast, to Dire Dawa and Addis Ababa. It carries coffee out of the country and brings cars and other **imports** in. But most things are moved by road.

Roads

Three things make it possible to move supplies and people over huge areas of desert and mountain. These are Ethiopia's expert drivers, skilled mechanics and improved roads. If you travel by bus in the central highlands it takes a long time to cover short distances because mile after mile of steep, hairpin bends take you down the side of one mountain and then up the next. The long-distance truck and bus drivers have to be able to steer the largest of vehicles across miles of dangerous bends, without skidding on rubble or mud. They also have to know how to drive across desert areas without getting stuck for many hours. Most drivers have to be mechanics too, so they can fix breakdowns in the middle of nowhere. Very few people own cars, most people use taxis or buses.

The national bus company Abessa (Lion) Buses, with the lion symbol on the side, can be seen all over the country. Addis bus station is always full of people meeting, parting, waiting. In the city itself people can hire minicabs or taxis. Despite the lack of private transport there are often traffic jams in Addis Ababa.

Animal transport

Most people living in the countryside have to walk to the nearest town on rough, untarmacked roads like those around Deder. But traders called nagadis, who travel around the highlands taking supplies such as salt and coffee to the villages, often use donkeys or mule trains. Some of them drive pick-up trucks that bump along the lanes and pick up people hitching lifts into town. **Pastoralists** rely on another form of transport. When they move from one place to another with their animals, they load their tents, mats and cooking pots onto the backs of their camels. Small children are carried on the camels' backs too. Everyone else walks.

A Somali family moves on with everything neatly packed onto the family camel.

Ethiopia

You will know by now that no one picture or image could possibly sum up the variety of peoples and places in Ethiopia. If you were going to select pictures from this book to use to say something about Ethiopia to a friend, which would you choose?

The images of Ethiopia on this page and the next are far from the everyday lives of ordinary Ethiopian people. Most of this book has told you about the daily lives of country people. But the images on these pages are images of the real Ethiopia too, and they are ones that you can sometimes see on your television screen.

◁ The Bob Marley Music Shop in Woldiya in Wollo. The Rastafarian religion started in Jamaica as a tribute to the proud tradition of free Ethiopia.

△ A Christian priest showing valuable crosses used in processions.

▷ The dramatic and beautiful Blue Nile Falls.

▽ Deratu Tulu winning the 10,000 metres gold medal at the Barcelona Olympics in 1992.

Ethiopian people would want other countries to notice and learn about their achievements and their culture. No one wants their country to be seen as one big problem by the rest of the world. Many Ethiopian people have had some very difficult times to face in recent years, but even during those times things about the country and its people have inspired other people too. The images here show the significant contribution by Ethiopians to world religion and sport.

Ethiopia

Glossary

Cash Crops Crops which are grown to be sold rather than eaten by the farmers themselves. Cash crops like coffee are often sold for **export** to other countries. But cash crops can include food crops like **teff** or vegetables which are taken to a nearby market or sold to traders for money.

Christians People who believe in Jesus as the son of God and read the Bible.

Derg A group of junior army officers who overthrew Haile Selassie in 1974 and set up a **socialist** government which was defeated in 1991.

Exports Goods sold and transported to other countries.

Famine An extreme shortage of food. Poorer people may starve and die because they can't grow or buy enough food. Richer people survive.

Food Aid Foodstuff, such as maize or wheat, given to people unable to produce enough food to eat for themselves. It is usually given by one country to another either directly or through the United Nations World Food Programme.

Franchized Transnational Companies, such as Pepsi Cola sell permission to local companies to produce or market their product.

Imports Goods bought in from other countries.

Injera A soft dark spongy bread made from **teff** flour or a mixture of whatever grain grows locally with teff. It looks like a brown crumpet, with holes across the surface.

Muslim Muslims follow the Islamic religion which was founded by the prophet Mohammed in the 7th century.

Nationalized Land and other resources, becomes nationalized if a government takes them out of private ownership and puts them under state, or public ownership.

Nomadic groups of people who do not make their homes in one place but move around over long distances, taking their homes and household goods with them.

Qu'ran The holy book of Islam, containing the revelation of God to Mohammed.

Pastoralists People who mainly depend on livestock to make their living. They use the milk, meat and blood of their animals for food. Other animal products, such as skins, are sold or used to make clothes, houses, tools and containers. Ethiopian pastoralists are **Nomadic**, so move around over long distances to find fresh grazing for their flocks.

Primary Industries Industries which extract raw materials, such as minerals, oil and gas, from beneath the earth's surface.

Service Cooperative A consumer association set up by the government so that people in country areas can buy things which used to be hard to get outside big towns.

Socialist Political belief that society should be organized to put the interests of the community first, rather than the individual and which puts ownership of production in state hands.

Sorghum A kind of grain which grows well in lower, hotter areas.

Teff A grain unique to Ethiopia and people's favourite grain for making **injera**. It grows best on middle slopes (Woyne Dega).

Transitional government Transition means a temporary period of change. This government which has ruled Ethiopia since the overthrow of the **Derg** regime, has promised that elections will be held in which the people of Ethiopia can decide who they want to govern them.

Tukul Small round houses made from eucalyptus wood frames, with thatched roofs.

Index

About Oxfam in Ethiopia

The international family of Oxfam organizations works with poor people and their organizations in over 70 countries. Oxfam believes that all people have basic rights: to earn a living, and to have food, shelter, health care, and education. Oxfam provides relief in emergencies, and gives long-term support to people struggling to build a better life for themselves and their families.

Since the famine of 1983-85, Oxfam UK and Ireland's programme in Ethiopia has concentrated on famine prevention, agricultural recovery, improved water supplies, and public health. Oxfam works with local groups, particularly of women and pastoralists, on programmes of health care, soil and water conservation, and on the improvement of drinking water systems. Following Ethiopia's years of civil war, Oxfam supports organizations working with war-affected people, such as civilians and ex-soldiers with disabilities. Oxfam also works to reduce the impact of possible future emergencies, mainly by holding emergency stocks and running a transport operation (jointly with Save the Children Fund), to improve emergency food distribution systems.

The publishers would like to thank the following for their help in preparing this book: Roger Naumann and the staff of the Oxfam Horn of Africa Desk; Liz Stone and the staff of the Oxfam office in Addis Ababa; the people of Deru Welteaa; the Oxfam photo library and Jenny Matthews; and Ali Brownlie, Oxfam Education advisor who commented on early drafts.

The Oxfam Education Catalogue offers a wide range of books and resources on economically developing countries and development issues. These materials are produced by Oxfam (UK and Ireland), by other agencies and by Development Education Centres. For a copy of the catalogue contact Oxfam, 274 Banbury Road, Oxford OX2 7DZ, phone (01865) 311311, or your national Oxfam office.

Photographic acknowledgements

The author and publishers wish to acknowledge, with thanks, the following photographic sources:

Nigel Crofton pp4, 7; Colorsport p29l; Ethiopian Airlines pp19, 26, 29r; Carol Lee/CAFOD p18; Nikki Marsh p6; all other photos are by Jenny Matthews.

Cover photograph Young girl from Tigray – Hutchison Library

Note to the reader - In this book there are some words in the text which are printed in **bold** type. This shows that the word is listed in the glossary on page 30. The glossary gives a brief explanation of words which may be new to you.

First published in Great Britain by Heinemann Library an imprint of Heinemann Publishers (Oxford) Ltd Halley Court, Jordan Hill, Oxford OX2 8EJ

OXFORD LONDON EDINBURGH MADRID ATHENS BOLOGNA PARIS MELBOURNE SYDNEY AUCKLAND SINGAPORE TOKYO IBADAN NAIROBI HARARE GABORONE PORTSMOUTH NH (USA)

© 1995 Heinemann Publishers (Oxford)

00 99 98 97 96 95
10 9 8 7 6 5 4 3 2 1

British Library Cataloguing in Publication Data

Grunsell, Angela
Ethiopia, – (Worldfocus Series)
I. Title II. Series
963

ISBN 0 431 07263 9 (Hardback)

ISBN 0 431 07262 0 (Paperback)

Designed and produced by Visual Image
Cover design by Threefold Design

Printed in Hong Kong

A 5% royalty on all copies of this book sold by Heinemann Publishers (Oxford) Ltd will be donated to Oxfam (United Kingdom and Ireland), a registered charity number 202918.